Florida and Other Waters

Timothy Robbins

Copyright© 2023 Timothy Robbins
ISBN: 978-81-19228-25-6

First Edition: 2023
Rs. 200/-

Cyberwit.net
HIG 45 Kaushambi Kunj, Kalindipuram
Allahabad - 211011 (U.P.) India
http://www.cyberwit.net
Tel: +(91) 9415091004
E-mail: info@cyberwit.net

Printed at Replika Press.

for Nguyen The Lan — Mike

Acknowledgments

Pennsylvania Literary Journal: "56 in 2020"

Oddball: "My Names"

Impossible Archetype: "Happily Misnamed"

Cholla Needles: "Ceramic Resurrection," "Beach and Aquarium," "Babel"

Hanging Loose: "My Favorite Love Story," "The Actor," "This Bird"

Main Street Rag: "Doing My Part"

Slant: "When I Am"

Better Than Starbucks: "Lovelier"

Illuminations: "Her Paintings, Her Father," "Hand to Mouth"

Cardinal Sins: "Degas and the Sale of My Boyhood Home"

Ethel Zine: "What's the Screwdriver For?"

Off the Coast: "Occasional Poem"

Contents

Needles

John was sleeping in the tent when Marc
ducked under a pine branch. John's snore
had gone mute with the dawn chorus and
now was a whisper in growing amber
warmth. To avoid a face-full of needles
while passing under a drooping limb, Marc
bowed as only primates can. John woke
long enough to touch the molted sleeping
bag. Nothing alarming. Marc's early walks
were as normal as breakfast. The stiff needles
against Marc's baby-fine hair might have
revived: his father's fingers (one slightly
curtailed by a saw) freeing his dandruff;
a guitarist's calluses caressing his scalp; the
guitarist's heart tapping the opposite of SOS
in his flattened ear; Isis drawing her fingers
through Horus's curls as he drinks from her
breast; Delilah toying with Samson's ringlets,
twining rest and pretense of regret. (Marc was
after all a comparative mythologist.) John's
dream started worrying before John did.
The needles were claws stirring up dust.
Through the dust Marc saw a dim clearing,
frayed lawn chairs, a sofa with mud upholstery,
beer cans squeezed to hourglass shape, sort of,
a knife that threw a flashlight's beam on
leaves and in eyes. When John, hastily dressed,
found Marc at last, his arms were around
his knees, his face, nowhere to be seen. He

had gone back to the first beating when even
his attackers were too young to understand
why he had to be beaten.

56 in 2020

I'm placing all my hope, laying
it like an Easter egg, in writers
and artists who were young and
handsome in 1970, thin and sick
and dead as drinking straws,
mostly from AIDS-related
pneumonia, by 1990. We
decorated them by dipping them.
You remember those tiny
pellets of dye and the wash of
pale colors they left on shells
and songs about life ever-
lasting sung while we waited
for the eggs to dry. They came
in many colors, none of which,
not even the white, was pale.
Some had curly black burning
bushes on their heads and eye-
brows as black and thick as the
frames of their glasses.
Some were as blond as Tab
Hunter. They liked the look of
their hair on the shoulders of
their embroidered peasant
blouses. They liked to show off
their yearbook selves in white
starched shirts and starched
crewcuts. Some had Afros so
great, their heads seemed like the

Afros' devoted disciples. You
remember how momentous it
felt: every ounce of control in
your three-foot-high, hard-to-
control body concentrated in
plump hands to convey the eggs
without dropping or crushing them.
Some whispered. Some
spoke just above a whisper,
fearing a whisper would burn
and a full voice turn
them to rabbits exposed on the
lawn. Some boomed like their
despised fathers. They made
poems out of punctuation,
pictures out of punctuation,
collages and comic books and
paintings that bloomed or
crumbled when touched. They
looked safe in clouds of plastic
emerald-green grass. This
year or next, one would go
unfound and we would learn
our first lesson in the stench of
decay. All of my hopes. They
are as close to me as I am
to myself, and as far.

My Names

My folks didn't know that the one
they didn't pick, that was foisted
upon us, a forgotten history, a
conviction or acquittal pronounced
in a dream trial for a dream crime
that erased itself like passion —
was a patronymic for Robin, a
diminutive of Robert. It's a stretch,
but since stretching is my chief
virtue, this accounts for the lack of
Roberts on my dad's side, which drew
me to a Bob for my first crush,
feeling it would seal the circle if
I brought him into the clan. (He
wasn't to be brought.) They claimed
no reason lay within the first and
the middle names. I didn't believe
them, thought they were hiding
something, till, at 54, I realized
Timothy and *Allen* were my choices,
my first verbal achievement — that
I was one of a rare breed of fetuses
who, for nine months, whisper our
names into a communicative dark.
I didn't choose by meaning. I chose
as one chooses clothes. (And what
could they have been hiding? A fairy-
foretold doom only those names could
thwart? Pick a curse. Assertiveness

always aimed inward. A tendency
to float away if no man, no hundred-
kilo bag of quicksand, pins me
down. The urge to mate under a
candle that drips lava, to gather
wool over a spindle completing
a spinning wheel or a three milliliter
barrel.) There was a nickname I
hated. When Dad said it, I would
throw my thirty pounds at his
laughing torso, flailing and striking
with my awkward palms. Maybe he
used it so often because my anger
was hilarious, and his need for
hilarity was imperious. Maybe he
wanted to teach me to fight back.
I thought of this for the first time
today, wading through the surrenders
that clutter my first half century.
Timothy Two Tittle. I believed the
moniker was meant to mock an
unseen deformity (two baby pricks
between my legs).

Babel

In Westwood, Mike numbered
streets and restaurants I named.
Number 37: The Den of Soothing
Sticky Rice. Number 4: Noodle
Planet orbiting and eclipsing us

once a week for a reasonable
price. Cafe Habibi — 89 — we
passed nightly, glancing in at
Persian Disco beats. We went
in once in the afternoon, first-

time-curious hookah smokers.
The walls were crowded with
written shouts of love, Habibi's
linguistic mates — Italian, French,
Japanese, even Vietnamese. Mike

(né Lan) nearly rolled off his
Arabian cushion when he saw,
"The word a hooker would use
for *Big Boy* in the pitch: *Me love
you long time tonight.*" Building

a shelter, yet making it organic,
often feels like exclaiming
laughable words in serious tones.
Still, sometimes *My Love!*
joins us on a common wall.

Happily Misnamed

In a way, the twenty minutes in his truck were
the best thing that night. No 'way' about it;
they were so good they expanded
exponentially — 400 — 1,600 — inward and
outwardly. And as they expanded, the limits
of meaning stretched and contorted like pleas
on the skin of a balloon being blown up by
the dad of a kid turning five. The vehicle's
forward drive was painless. It was mastery that
didn't call attention to itself, didn't need its ego
propped up, its virility extolled to the heavens
of a lowered ceiling. The wait at the stoplights
was as filling as moments when an unhurried
man pauses inside you, his flesh contemplating
your depth — for he turned and looked at me
as he spoke, and we saw the light change on
each other's cheeks, night's approval altering
our complexions, hinting at newly tinted races.
The mission was practical: Find an all-night drug-
store and spirit away condoms and lube. "We are
an Arabian prince and a Persian peasant
questing for Ali Baba's cave, risking life and
freedom on a life-changing lamp." He smirked,
wagged his head and said, "Shit, you're
the literary type. Damn, that's hot." And as though
it were predictable foreplay, we were suddenly
talking about his mother, who loved to read and
had named him for her favorite novel, for his
name was not what his text had claimed. He was

the handsome, ageless — elite, heartless Dorian
Gray. "It doesn't suit you," I said." The drugstores
were dark; his need was not soon to be sated;
his hidden painting would go unscarred.

Ceramic Resurrection

Beth gave us the mixing bowls, the
best breed of offhand bequeathal,
before the basement was filled
with pancake batter and cement.

One yellow as a faded apron,
the other green as the ground on
which Alice challenged the Mad
Hatter. It was before the house

rose like the black bits of dead
Voldemort, as though the House
of Usher had gotten religion,
the old time-iest, and was making

the timeliest conman's escape.
Green fit in Yellow as no mama's
boy ever fit his mama's lap.
Green and Yellow were as simple

as eggs except for their lip
and resonance when tapped. Eggs
were as simple as Yellow and
Green except for their jagged edges

when halved. It was the longest
basement I ever trod, dim and
redolent of sod and wood aging
more gracefully than nations.

The smallest queen, she led and
gestured right then left, each
gesture an offer, and spoke of
her husband hollowing out a

hangar, and art quilts growing in
her studio deep as snow, and
the heifer who calved and crow
fledglings eaten below the

upturned hat where they hatched.
Hat or bowl? It was before God's
right hand turned out to be a
spatula he used to sever and serve

the screened-in porch that dared
the lake that thought it was dawn
though we believed it was night.
Now bowl sits within bowl on

shelf above radio and I think how
everything fits inside another thing,
as I wash and dry and sing a
descant over endless bad news.

My Favorite Love Story

Joan Crawford called Billy Haines and
Jimmie Shields Hollywood's Oscar-
worthy marriage. Every time I misquote
her I wish I knew when she first said it.
Was it before Billy told Louis B. Mayer,
"I'll leave Jimmie when you leave your
wife," turned on the heels of sharp shoes
I picture with spats and stepped (*allegro*)
away from top billing, from any billing
before Mayer could shut his mouth? Was
it at the soirée Miss Crawford staged
for the interior Billy made for her? I
picture the Art Deco set of "The Artist,"
Joan unrolled beside elongated white
statue hounds, dictating with a pair of
silver tongs. It could have been any time
after final credits rolled, first on Billy,
then on Jimmie. I defend — I extol him
for following Billy like an erstwhile
Hindu widow in a tranquil rewrite of Sati.
Mike (14 years my junior) says he won't
stick around if I go first. I think of
Jimmie's last note seeking his friends'
forgiveness and — wholeheartedly —
I grant it.

The Actor

He was with me because I resembled
his mark, and his stage training had
etched in him the importance of
blocking. He was endearingly pretentious
about the subtext he brought to his
roles. Gazing at a female love interest,
he was a blind man praying to the
mirror that restores sight. Ogling a
male love interest, he was the oldest
Magi, the one who traveled furthest.
He played a drug overlord's faithful
lieutenant as a housewife Saran-
wrapping brownies for the church bake
sale. His fathers were old houses with
roofs that leaked for spite and found-
ations with puzzling low self-esteem.
His mothers were condos so decorated
there was no place left to hang. His
sons and daughters were tents that held
only the essentials. (When pressed, he
listed toothbrush, twink and bong.)
His librarian constantly shushed quiet
readers. Her untamed heart was
a goat grazing, screaming in her throat.
When we met he was playing a flight
attendant in town for a few hours,
scoring meth at a bath house. He saw
himself step into a bus and look back
at me to see if I was the emergency

exit or a safe window that might reflect
lines he had flubbed. I was happy
when he spoke in a mashup of speeches
from his parts. He was sure then. // He
squanders his days debating
what to do with his new sight. Watch
for fires from a high solitude? Search
for new stars? Become his generation's
foremost online voyeur? Bask in sun-
light or shun it? Always wear goggles? //
In bed, where deep sleep and dreams
are event horizons, all argument ends
in homecoming. I knew it was no star
we were following. I knew the others
knew this too. I knew the babe would
be like any other, a rhythm of quiet
and noisy selfishness. I knew I'd be
lucky to make it to Bethlehem and
only a miracle would return me home.
This is why I did it: to die in motion,
hopefully a meteor, not a meteorite. //
He'd never made brownies. No one
made them in the house where he
grew up. He didn't reject the church.
He never considered it. His dedication
to backstory ended where work started.
There would be no baking. No baptism.
He imagined the brownies came out
hard and that Cartel Mom chuckled
thinking of church ladies chipping
their teeth. // I used little imagination
on the parents because I am not and
never will be one. // He stuck me in

the past with card catalogues, cards that
I had to fill out by hand. I'm a slut and
not a good-looking one. No glasses to
take off, no bun to shake into bouncing
tresses. He thinks he's done something
brilliant, making me the opposite of my
stereotype. Destruction delineated by a
fire brake. Sugar cane stripped before
harvest. A harvest of toxins hanging
below the lowest clouds. // That I never
saw him blush isn't strange. How
often do we pink up from shame? How
often does rage redden the face? His
acting laugh was natural. He could usually
cry when the script said to. Movie-
goers, I can vouch for his sex scenes'
grunts. No, I never saw him blush.
The time he said, "If I could blush on
cue I'd be the greatest," was the only
time I felt him sigh.

This Bird

There are those birds. They're as unwilling
to be seen as signals that shoot from
the remote to the TV, a one-way discussion.
They have no names, at least not yet. Then
there are those birds as tight and warm as a
young runner's skin, as tight and cold as
a frozen river. They are called, respectively,
the bird that doesn't sing but pants and
the bird that tries but fails to deliver.
There are those birds. Their names are as
un-hide-able as bellies about to give birth.
They are Eagles, Falcons, Swans, Sun,
Moon and even the Earth. They enter
between the marathon runner's shoulder
blades and exit through his or her sternum as
fast as a clap. They make truckers drive so
hard their rubber pulls the road up behind them.
Those birds have no subtlety. Not this bird.
I won't say this bird's name. You may know
him by another, and more than I wish
for the return of my favorite broken-up
band, more than I wish for Siri to stop
responding to the accidental brush of the
side of my hand on her button, I wish for
you not to be confused. I don't want you
to think: *That bird he talks about with such
rapture and insight, it has nothing to do
with the bird I hear outside my window.*
This bird is well rested. He's not up

before dawn like those frantic robins that
think night is a fire that has blackened
their feathers forever. This bird is sensible
about his glasses. When they break, he
makes of them splints and crutches for
birds — and other creatures! — who
have fallen into the clutches of Old
Man Injury. This bird is incisive. He
uses two notes and would use one were
it not for the prejudice that insists:
The repetition of one note is not singing.
Yes, it appalls him. But he knows his
singing will help no one if he's the only one
who knows it is song. The thought of this bird
is stubborner than the eyes in the mantel
paintings in haunted houses in silly movies —
for this thought follows you wherever
you go *and* wherever you do not. This bird
will make google eyes at you if that's
what it takes. He will transform himself into
the drinking bird on your grandmother's shelf
above the sink, forever trying to slake its
thirst though it knows it cannot drink through
its plastic beak — not even if you sneak in
at night and make a hole in it. Just as he goes
on dipping an dipping, I could go on
ripping off and ripping off the mystical
poets and the manufacturers of kitsch —
but will say just one thing more. I know
you will try to bribe me, force me, trick me
into revealing this bird's name. You
might as well lock that door and burn it.
I won't reveal the secret, even if this bird
himself, implores me to do it.

Doing My Part

The assignment Mom gave me: to help
Dad make up his mind, a task at which,
it seems, he has become much better
or much worse. Either could account
for his refusal to declare his plans.
Is the delay a gift — be it horse or
other beast — from the long Covid
shutdown? Or is the journey itself the
mouth into which, he feels, it would be
offensive to look? Not that sensitivity
is new to him, but could the unrest for
which we will be remembered have
rendered his consideration for others
crippling? Or his consideration for his
own feelings clandestine? I find myself
replaying what he said when I announced
my love for men. No, announcement's
not the right word. It was more like an
Annunciation, the hushed, firm speaking
of an inevitable haiku. "We knew and
we're happy you…" His delivery and
timing, neither rushed nor reluctant,
were perfect. Clearly the fruit had been
ripe for some time, and the challenge
had been how to stop it from spoiling.
Also — it occurs to me for the first time —
he was being practical — as I should
be now. It's June 27th and Mom wants
to be here by mid-July. By *here*, she

means the hotel downtown, on the Lake,
twenty steps from Common Grounds
(a coffee house), a stone's stroll to any
antique shops that managed to skip
along the water. She means our driveway,
where we'll stand pressed together like
praying hands while my husband and
hers tilt, still charmingly awkward
after 23 years.

When I am

When I am better at making my mind go blank;
when my step and clutch on metal ladders
bolted to metal walls are surer; when I'm reliably
inspired to seek secret drawers, violate
them and interpret their contents;
when I love my forehead's lines as faithfully
as they love me; when I convince you
that rivers of rippling water and rivers of
rippling moths both seek the same lost stuff
and it's not the sea though the sea is what they
find; when I dedicate the spells of every
witch to one task alone and if that task is to
guide lost children home; when I wield the
eloquence that convinced the Phoenicians
to tar their warships pink and when I wield it
against all of War's toys — then will I deserve
yours or any girl's or boy's loving trust.

Lovelier

Gerardo lives with 18 bikes, three of them
tandems, one of the tandems his favorite,
he can't say why. It's not the one he rides
most. To the most-ridden he has attached
a child's carseat. Papa, eight- and two-year-
old *mijos* fulfill its needs conquering and
reconquering Kenosha's parks on a regular
rotation. I've seen pictures of the bikes in
his garage that looks like a 19th century shop,
mostly dim with flashes here and there like
silver finches searching for an exit. I've
seen the three tandems posing with the three
riders, whose stiff smiles hide the delight
they must feel when they become a small,
perfect parade moving away from the wife
and mother who itches to clear the garage
in their absence. A lovelier sight? Can't
think of one. Not even the Turkish gymnast
with eyebrows as dark, as thick, as solemn
as I drew them when he begged (yes, it
surprised me too) for a portrait. Not even
the last sight of the house I grew up in —
every part of it fixed, the basement air
breathable, the cracks in the plaster painted
over — every room as empty as a soul that
never hurt, transitively or intransitively.
What is Gerardo? What are his sons, who
stare at the back of his head? Their voices,
even when Gerardo twists around, are

mostly carried off by the wind. What will
happen if the sons tire of Gerardo's constant
leadership; if the baby sprouts wings, breaks
free of his safety restraints and flies cloud-
ward; if the middle rider faints toward the
pedals or leaps to the road? What promise
will be broken or kept if they never tire?

Her Paintings, Her Father

Her paintings, when she unveiled
them for her father, were propped
in wooden chairs, upright and

stiff, a family whose perfect
posture and prolonged effort to
be quadrilateral had earned them

a place under sheets. She was let
down when he didn't gasp, or turn
his head or even frown. When

canvases burning in the driveway,
threatening to reignite dawn, lit
her face and his back, she knew

she had won. Later, when he was
cremated, she thought: *No need to
look, I've already seen.*

Hand to Mouth

"That chair looks good in your sweater."
I love that line. I know it's mine but can
not remember where, when, why it came
to me. I like to think of it as a sudden
sketch of Ichabod Crane who has just
claimed the aisle-half of the Muni love-
seat where I'm bent over a broken paper-
back. His eyes grin through the lenses of
his pince-nez (I chose that because I've
never actually seen one) as I scan the car
for a cardigan-draped chair. I spy many
empty loveseats and my eyes join his grin.
I disembark at the United Nations Plaza
stop. The third time this week, a woman
surrounds me. Hard to believe one woman
can surround anybody so thoroughly, let
alone a woman so small and neat. She's a
fully blossomed flower of the Reverend
Sun Myung Moon. (See her unblooming
a little in the dim of an unreverend moon.)
She is hunting men's heads for a mass
wedding, hopes to fill her quota soon,
shadows then passes me to her sister. This
time, prepared to compete, I join in, "I too
hunt men's heads on the street. I too can
never have enough husbands!" One lift
later, in the teachers' lounge, George and
I laugh about it. "George," I remark, "Your
chair looks good in that sweater." "Ah,

you know I can't resist such utterances!
Is it a pickup, an insult, a koan? Is it work-
place harassment that coyly stops just
short of the line?" In those days, George
was a plump fearless Buddhist, Gay in
the San Francisco and Bing Crosby way.
Last night I dreamed of him as he is now,
a faint white light in a paper lantern. He
floated along Market Street, bouncing on
chair, good and *sweater* — a sing-along
ball. He was taken up by Moonie maidens
who passed him along like a hero or a
shared burden. And I recalled what had
been lost in funny retellings: *Sir, are you
single and lonely?* Thus their pitch began.

Degas and the Sale of My Boyhood Home

Degas before a bulldozed lot
stares at a house he once
lived in. A fresh morbid thought
splashes in the shower as I
squirt too much shampoo on

my palm: What if David, whom
time has turned to my most
loyal friend, goes before I go?
Degas guesses who sits —
and why is she looking up? —

at the third-story window.
There's a crane on a square
crater's rim in downtown
Chicago. This crane thinks
little of its strength, preferring

to bemoan lack of grace
relative to Degas's creakiest
dancer. Degas feels no
sympathy, his view blocked
by ravished eyes and the

bitterness of a thousand
uncompromising portraits.
I weld a camera to an
excavator's claw and market
the film as the history of

my halting artistry. Degas
hands me his pocket watch
and asks me to walk the dog.
He hands me his yoyo and
asks what time it is and if

the cafe is open yet. The
sound of my man's sleep
is Duncan, which is to say
it's either or it's both the
sound of a yoyo rolling down

and climbing up its string or
a string banishing and
recalling its yoyo. An
extravagant way of praising
the fickleness of the sound

of his sleep. Affidavit —
sounds like a flower — petals
a color that strikes the eye
as good cold coffee strikes the
tongue. My neighbor promised

me a start from her affidavits.
She's so busy, she's probably
forgotten. Maybe I should
slip over and help myself.
Degas stares, satisfied, at a

canvas he worked on for
years and I painted over last
night. "Here lies my judgment,"

he says. "I won't miss it. So
often it misled me." True. His

guesses were wrong. Dreyfus
and twenty other Jews, my
man and I, my parents, their
vigor, the people who bought
56 years from them — and yes,

a handful of retired ballerinas
crowd at that honest window.
Desperate to see one last
pirouette, Degas commands
us to whisper and jump.

What's the Screwdriver for?

A tiny screwdriver rests on the sill
between the sink and days of outside waving.
It's the size of a surgical instrument for
miniature automatons. But don't waste your
first guess on that. Automatons and
homophobes are the only life forms
not found in our home. It's here the dishes
and I exchange secrets; here I reassure them
we won't accept the kitchenware my
mother's tired of. "It's finer than ours,"
I concede, practicing my retail voice, "but it
isn't ours." We want the plates on which,
on the 11th of September, we ate but didn't
taste Mike's sister's crumbling panettone;
the plates we pushed away ten years later
when our country's gloating over an enemy
killed our appetites and we hoped that
counted as fasting. These mugs from the
Indoor Opossum Association, these Chinese
bowls stained like dentures in a Polident
commercial, this stoneware that conspires
with the microwave to burn our forgetful
fingers — they've heard all the updates
of my pet names for him — as hard to
keep up with as new software — while
his "Hey Mister" for me remains constant —
a drone, a flatline. In this dainty teacup we
served Helen from the Health Department.
The Oolong cooled as the interview wore

on and the room darkened like the set of an
avant-garde one-act play far far off Broad-
way. It closed after one performance and we,
the stars, repaired to a quiet cast party that
continues to this day. They heard me
marvel at the abundance of Wisconsin
willows that strike me as graceful like Hula
dancers, not lachrymose; while he insisted
he's untouched by sunrise beauty, which
is true most of the time but occasionally,
like a flare shot by a cop or a hiker stranded on
an outcrop, is not. They were here when
he recognized every face but Albert Finney's
no matter how much the face was changed
by age or depression, lack of an Oscar
or lack of a blockbuster. No matter how
brief the glimpse. How we sighed and laughed —
if only eye witnesses were that reliable. They
hear us improvise thunderingly orchestrated
preludes to hushed apologies. They hear
the tales of his nieces and nephews —
she who wanted a pineapple for her birthday
(she had drawn everything else); he who
wanted an egg for Christmas (no one knew why
though it was clear he repeated the request
when he saw how it amused the grown-ups);
she who, not understanding the family is rich,
helpfully offered to sell bracelets in the park.
Oh the devotion to worry that runs in the family.
Mike insisted on chauffeuring me to work
in the wake of the alleged fake assault
on Jussie Smollett. The plates were here
in 2008. In the middle of a November night
we saw Indiana briefly blaze blue and he

learned the expression 'blue blazes.' Christ-
mas morning 2019 they heard the first
reading of *A Day in the Life of Marlon Bundo.*
In the eleven years between he licked himself
lean as Jack Sprat, and his mom and I
feared an eating disorder. Meanwhile my
face grew soft and headed south and I
offended time by trying to adjust my neck and
mouth — even bought from Amazon a face
tightening gadget. I learned that grinding
and brewing his coffee while he sleeps beats
a priest's preparations for the Mass. We went
through all the poems in which he appeared
as *you,* changing the *you's* to *he's* to make
sure no reader could squeeze free of truth's
loose grip. I took to carrying a travel size
Scope. (He insists kisses must stay fresh
as hope.) All the while that screwdriver has
served us well, and that brings me to the point.
If you think you know what it's for, send email
to <u>toolsoflife@hotmail.com</u>. First prize:
someone, sometime, some home.

Beach and Aquarium

I read an account of a shark who
finds itself the center of unwanted
attention, the guy I've seen in
old movies who blunders onto

a stage where he doesn't belong.
But the shark enjoys one lucky
mercy: being dead, it doesn't feel
curious hands, cautiously prodding

toes, innocent and yet untoward
caresses. In a salty rush, a sleek
stingray glides through memory's
warm water, through the depth of

a kiddy pool with its consequent
clarity, alarming or reassuring
depending on the water's specs,
in this case determined by wise

policy and profit motive. "Dangle
your hand," say signs and docents.
"They will come to you," and
they do — supple and docile

as house cats, rubbery flying
shower mats. As they're flat, you
need a moment to see: it's the
same point on the cat's forehead,

the spot where Hindu women
dab their red, that seeks your
fingertips. "Don't be afraid,"
the docent says to the nervous

kid beside you while a small ray,
maybe a child itself, rises to your
wiggling touch, life's fearless-
ness saluting life's hesitancy.

Florida

What a world. In minutes
I learn that in December
1947 *Hoosier Folklore*,
a publication of Indiana University,
my alma mater twice over,
printed three versions of
the cumulative story
"There Was an Old Lady who
Swallowed a Fly."
In minutes, the journal
with its elderly Coloradan,
Georgian, and Buckeye fly-eaters
graced my Mac screen.

An issue of Foxfire Magazine
with its bear-brown cover,
its body warped and stiffened
page by page,
its instructions for sewing
an Appalachian dulcimer —
I rescued it from a Friends
of the Library sale,
lugged it around for a few
undergrad years
before failing it as it failed me.

The song tickled when
I was young. An adult, I believed its
wisdom.

*We are live in Miami with what doctors are
saying about variants BA4 and BA5.*

*After two years I got it in April. But it
wasn't bad. It's like the flu in that it's out there.*

*People come in for something different
and find out they've got it.*

*ABC Local 10 News.
Most cases are mild but deaths
are still happening.*

*Today we went to all the government-run
testing and treatment sites in Jacksonville.
There are only three left and at two of them,
well, we found no patients.*

*Popular Radio Host of WJCT
self-quarantined. A fresh verb in the c.c..
At Baptist Health, 75 cases, seven in ICU.
(Governor, I see you.)*

*If I get Corona, I get Corona. At the end
of the day, I'm not going to stop partying.
We've been waiting for Miami Spring Break
for a long time — for two months!*

*What is there to do here besides go
to the bars and beach? And they're
closing it all. It's really messed up.
We need a refund.*

There's more serious things out there
like hunger and poverty.

You have to let go and let God. But
what I don't like is pastors who
endanger their congregations — their livelihoods.

I see EMS stretchers all down
the block. There is physically no more room
in the Emergency Room. It feels like you're
standing on the shore of a tsunami and
FEMA is offering you a life
preserver.

You can actually see those cloudy
patches on their lungs mature in real time.
So let's think about this.

The building is on fire. We are all fire fighters
inside trying to put it out. But we're naked.

Haines City in Polk County.
Population 13,174 in 2000,
which Mom, Dad and I rang in
in San Francisco in a studio
on Taylor Street. We went to bed
early, I on the floor, they on
the futon we brought home
on a bus. Mike had just started
grad school at UCLA ("Ookla"
my Italian students would say).
In New Year's Eve dark,
I sang, "Unhappy Days
are Here Again. Skies Above
and Below are Drear Again."
Should I move to L.A.? "That
seems best," Dad counseled.
Haines City, 20,535 souls in 2010,
my parents among the newcomers.
Mike and I were in Ann Arbor.
Back to the homey Midwest,
for me. First time beyond a
Metropolis for him.
Named for a Confederate
Colonel, formerly home to
Circus World, then Boardwalk
and Baseball, H.C. grows
thanks to Orlando. This
project will work if I tap into other
minds. If I siphon off (ease the
tube down Granddad's throat —
just opened his throat and

swallowed a goat) gallons of
Granddad's gasoline wine.
Florida springs from the state's:
oldsters from the North, tourists
from everywhere and
Deepest Southerners
of various complexions —
plus more recent immigrants
with various connections; from
dementia, relaxation, death and
death's delay, anxiety about
grandkids, indifference to grandkids,
repetition and shuffling.
Breakfasting on oranges.
Dining on glistening barbecue.
Feeling as satisfied — as self-
satisfied as a mandarin pierced
by a straw (Stomach and
Conscience debate the cause
of the price hike
of gasoline wine).
But most of all Beauty.
Most of all Madness.
Most of all Redundancy.
My first morning there, a mocking-
bird groused about tap water that
tastes like sulfur,
Unions that blow away like chalk,
a governor who talks with chalk
on his lips, fish that climb out
of ponds and walk to pools; walk to
gated enclaves where rich
retirees hatch burdensome

voting rules; walk to hospitals
where Liberty in a wheelchair
cheers and drools.
Most of all the bird complained
about complaints.
Then it fell quiet
and after a while, sang of
cranes and herons and doctors
and nurses and the Florida
Scrub Jay and the Northern
Cardinal; sang beautifully of
these and other saints.
My parents consult their
mockingbird as faithfully as they
listen to gossip and weather
warnings and rumors of arcane short-
cuts that bypass toll roads.
"How do you know it's the moc-
kingbird and not a mourning dove
or an egret or a wood stork?"
"Because it's a mourning
dove and an egret and a wood stork
in rapid succession from the same tree."
"And how do I know it's you and
not the mockingbird telling me so?"
Her answer: an exasperated
kiss on my cheek. She's in the breakfast
nook, hypnotizing her second cup,
hypnotized by an Alphabet Mystery book
while Dad does the dishes.
I take a picture of her from behind:
a polar bear dowager queen
in a white bathrobe. I text

the photo to Eco-warrior friends with the
caption: *Polar Bear in Haines City —
talk about immigration.* She's
upset when I show her the pic.
(Warrior text back: at some
point you won't joke; at some
point you won't wake from the
dream in which the last polar
bears swim through our
last bloodstream.) "I look like
an old lady." I feel bad.
I know how she feels.
I've just gotten over my frustration
at no longer being the winsome
lad my husband fell in love with
25 years ago. I thought that
frustration would be with me till
the last stop. But it got off some-
where between Kenosha and Miami
and hasn't been heard from since.
Unless it's one of those walking
fish that somehow made it over the
electric fence only to be swallowed —
whole — by an alligator.
Syphon and channel. I've got my
own bad hearing — tinnitus
plus no high pitches in my left ear
engenders endless comical mis-
hearings. But they are mine, not
Dad's or Granddad's. Somehow
I must scrunch down in their
middle ears, snuggle up to their
auditory nerves and mishear as Dad

and his Dad do. *There was an*
old ear that swallowed a sound.
Puget Sound? Mistakes abound.
Once Granddad told me, as if in
confidence, "No wonder there are so
many plane wrecks. There's only
one control tower for all the airports
in the country." Then, reading
my face, "I know. I was shocked
too. But I heard it. I heard it on
the news last night." And then
there was the time my dad heard
on *CBS Sunday Morning:* "Me
and Bobby McGee" was written
for the late, great Jimi Hendrix
(who shouted, "Scuse me while
I kiss this guy!" — not, as
everyone thinks, "Scuse me
while I kiss the sky!")
And the time Mom lamented
the 10,000 people who move to
Florida every week.
"No wonder you can't drive
through Walmart without getting into
a traffic jam." Aisles are art-
eries clogged with plaque.
One control tower for all my
emotions. For every decision
I regret, though I assert I don't
indulge in regret. One for each
of the the five types of poem
I write. For my sexual
responses. For traps I

swallow to catch guys.
I swallow guys to stroke their thighs.
I stroke their thighs to elicit
their sighs. I elicit their sighs
to hoist myself to the skies.
But who knows why I
want to be hoisted?
Especially with just one air
traffic control tower in play.
No, my Hoosier mom is
not pretty anymore. Not like she
was in front of the first trailer,
a mother at 21 in a Decatur County
Village; in front of the Methodist
parsonage; in front of the
congregation, singing
with a voice I can't remember
and no one recorded. Still,
she's beautiful in her fake
polar bear coat with Florida
morning sun docking like
a great white boat, rustling like
a bridal gown, sitting by her son,
who is flecked with color
like an artist's smock.
The watch she keeps on the sandhill
cranes and their annual chick —
twins this year —
is beautiful. She thinks:
I was a good parent — but not
like that. I had other responsibilities
whereas these birds are literally
full-time. Yet, last summer the

gator that eyes Dad when he
fishes; that eyes the golfers when
they descend from their carts
to make great sweeping arcs
with ridiculous scythes —
erased the baby bird in a flash of
rugged hide. That evened
the parenting score.
This year they are four and they
strut on their folding stilts (see
the golfers swing, choreographed
by Buzz Berkeley while the gators
sing, "It don't mean a thing
if you ain't got that…" dodging
falling golfballs).
I know an old woman who
swallowed a crane. She gulped
the crane to transmute the pain.
Bird-eating as alchemy.
Mom reclines in the Florida
room, where observation of
creatures so like her, so unlike her,
transmutes a meaningless
empty hour into a meaningful
empty hour. She thinks out loud,
"We could learn something from
their gait. Golfers who can't
find their balls (take that as you
will) could learn from their
foraging. The gators could learn
from their childrearing.
A lot of couples I know could
learn from their loyalty

(not the same as fidelity).
My son could learn from their
unseen creativity." What could they
learn from us? Knowledge of Beauty.
Adam Crane and Eve Crane eat
the forbidden beetle and the world
around them is alchemized;
It's like being driven from one young-
folks home to another. I know an old
woman (my grandma) who refused
to swallow anything. The doctors
sedated her before easing
the tube down her throat to —
what is the opposite of syphon?
She swallowed the tube to stay alive.
But of course that's wrong.
She had mated for life with her mind,
but now her mind had left her,
depriving her of any future 1st
person singular utterance that ended
with an infinitive of purpose. The sun
rose to justify extravagant claims
about Florida sunrises. The sun
set to do as much. Intense red
 and orange touched the sky
wherever they could. They
stretched the sky so they could
touch more. Purple as deep as
 the Devil's birthmark appeared
to remind us of Evil. Blue as
black as night painted
prophecy on the clouds.
Blue as black as night lingered

on the clouds. A force like a
steam locomotive carried pink light.
There was monstrous dew.
Dew drowned rodents. Dew
rivaled handheld mirrors.
Dew told tall tales.
Dew made an audible splash
when it broke on the pavement.
Dew fell like spiteful rain on
the gong-like parts of cars
left in driveways. "You've
 never seen anything like it,
have you?" Dad said with disgust.
"Why spend money on bottled
water when you can harvest
this ripe swollen fruit?" I suggested.
"It's a pain in the neck," he said.
"We can't leave anything
out overnight." What do they
want to leave out overnight?
Fat cushions? Books? Resolutions
to do better, to waste less, to
keep their tempers when the
world gets even wetter?
Unwanted furniture and the
unwanted people who sit on it —
that's a different matter.
Behold sun rays slanting in
at a Floridangle — a spotlight
on the Surfside Condominium
Collapse. I'm looking at a photo
I'd like to use for the cover
 of this book-length (I hope)

poem. On the left, Champlain's
 undamaged block looms
at an Expressionist angle.
It remains attached like
a Siamese twin to the central
building, part of which is
still whole, while part has
been ripped into Expressionist lace
that spills into a mound of gray
detritus in the foreground.
In the background, glimpses
of water are the color of a
plum, pallid with terror.
Two spotlights from helicopters
are frozen in their nosy rove
over this architectural corpse.
What pulled these homes down
like flimsily mounted shelves?
The Floridamned dew,
Floridayrise light. "The Democrats'
socialism and pederasty,"
growls the governor. There are
rumors of a prophet who was
ignored — and underpaid.
There are reports as old as Isaiah
of greedy, shortsighted companies.
Video that shows what looks like
Pan on a kiteboard riding a
breaking crest of concrete was
suppressed. In Dad's book
nothing shows bad character
like shoddy workmanship.
This will work if I syphon —

I can put my mouth on the
gassy tube or with a second tube
and a cloth keep my lips pure —
questionable fuel. At some
point, there will be fire
extinguishers on every tree trunk.
At some point the Northern Cardinals
will rely on them. At some
point grand-parental bones
lash out at their own fat deposits.
Liposuction without surgery,
a sort of "weight-lifting" contest.
At some point cameras will
piggyback on trees. At one
point Mother Crane with her
beak like a table knife
carves a snake into chick-
sized bites for her chick.
When she gets to the tail,
the swallowing gets rough
and Mother's attempts at
force feeding are futile.
Father Crane fetches a wet
spider and Mother Crane
sings, "I know a brave chick
who swallowed a spider
that wriggled and jiggled in a
soon-to-be lengthy throat."
In a seed town in the Panhandle
family, pastor and congregation
shovel Jesus, servitude and
skirts — recipes and boys
down a girl's throat. The only

way she can think to stop
the forced feeding is to swipe
the rope coiled in the canoe,
to uncoil and recoil it
around her windpipe, tight. At
one point in this composition,
the mockingbird switched from long
to short lines — to evoke his grand-
hen's and grand-cock's emaciation.
To evoke the westside stretch
of Florida's section of I75.
To evoke what MLK called
the Long Arc of History, which
I think is more like an unrolling
skein of yarn. (Wishful un-skeining?)
Mom was as fit as a dress-form.
Dad was track-runner skinny,
cruciform. Still the trailer must
have felt cramped even before
my brother and I came along.
This was in Indiana, but might
as well have been in the Pan-
handle for Billy Lucas, who also
used rope — in his grandma's barn.
That was 2013 in my hometown.
Mike and I had just moved from
Ann Arbor to Kenosha.
My parents' third time wintering
in a rental in Haines City.
The next year they bought a 'unit'
smaller than the trailer they
started out in before Kennedy
was POTUS or POTUS was shot.

The water heater could handle
one shower per morning. So
Dad and I used the shower
house. I got lost coming back
at 3:00 a.m. and wandered the
park for two hours before
recognizing telltale yellow
lawn table and chairs. It was
frustrating to the point of tears
in the surprisingly cold dark
(with hair wet). Later it was
alchemized into a welcome
boost to my reputation as one
who can get lost in his own
clothes. Central Park 1 —
CP1 then CP 2. There the
manufactured house
was like a real home with
two baths and a grown-up
water heater. A fine place
for paradise parents to host
their gaggle of long-time
Hoosier friends turned snowbirds,
plus all the friends from CP1,
many of them Canadian, plus
the more affluent new neighbors.
I, with my wonderful hermit
husband, with friends scattered
like birdseed under far-flung
feeders, envied them. A hurricane
of sociability and Mom and Dad in
the storm's eye devoid of
background noise so even

Dad needed no hearing aid.
Three years of that. Then
various Bonnies and Daves,
Johns and Deannas got gout
in their wings, which stopped
their flying south. Others died
outright and the drive from
the Midwest to the deepest
South felt more and more
like they were cattle driven
by old age's drover.
They betrayed their house
of 50 years, betrayed my
childhood (you see,
I'm not even trying to
excuse my feelings about
this) and moved to a new
proper home on a golf course
in one of those enclaves. Unit:
How to talk to the demented
Crane? Slowly, the way it steps
through blades of grass almost
as long and almost as thin as its
leather-stick legs with the
ankle knot that most non-bird
bipeds mistake for knees.
Patient as a hungry gator.
Oh, that's the patience I envy.
Slowly and a little bit at a time.
Unit: When to swallow
the blue pill? The next day.
When to sic the green pill
on the blue? Unit: And there's

Bonnie, who got so mad
at tenants whose dogs shit so
peacefully on her lawn.
One day she visited *their* lawn,
pulled her sweatpants down
and shit on the dandelions.
Now pantsing herself, going
down on her haunches,
shitting inside or out — she
needs help. Unit: And there's
Steve, infamous Lothario,
 impressive at his age.
Fornication that would
otherwise be condemned, is
winked at. Why? Because he
looks after Phil, who trembles
so kite-like, so sheet-on-the-
line-like. FloriDaddy and his
Floridalliances. Unit:
Mother Crane used to tan her
plumage with orange mud,
as if she weren't already
happily wed to the wetlands.
Her once artistic bill is even
clumsier than her chick's when she
taught him the skill. "The guilt!"
she cries in the guttural speech
of Cranes. Whatever she had to
say, she used to say it to whatever
was above her, straightening her
supple neck like the handle
of a rake. Now she speaks
to her breast feathers, too weak

to stretch or seeking protection
where her chick once sought it.
Trailers lit for Christmas.
Ambulance lights, but quiet,
as even glaring light likes to be.
The contest of the lights.
The prize? That we not back-
track into the dark. That we
embrace individual liberty for
everyone, not just for ourselves.
That we never get stuck-up
or strung up. Let Jesus apologize
for bringing a sword, not peace.
Let him disavow that remark
and swan-trumpet, Gabriel-trumpet:
Peter, sheathe that damn thing.
No one's born in these enclaves.
Every few months someone dies.
Bonnie the friendly Hoosier
with the twinkle in her eyes.
"Term limits" doesn't necessarily
mean she condones assassination
of duly elected officials but
when she describes this,
there's that twinkle again.
If this is really going to work,
eventually we have to re-drive
the long bright road to Uncle
Ray's house. The long dark road
back. Oncoming headlights
rearing up from the Void.
Ray dancing his way to Charlene
on a clubfoot, the Great Depression,

idylls of Greensburg, war in
Germany, first marriage, working
for RCA, spreading television
sets (riddle me this: *How
is a TV set like a sunset?*) like
chicken feed. A separate song for
Ray and Charlene and the omens
 that were their big spirits.
At a gathering with relatives
I didn't know, Charlene alone
understood: The way to ease me
out of my shyness was not to blast
me with a spotlight (I'm no rubble;
I hoard no dead bodies).
For shy folks, a spotlight is
an interrogation light.
She asked me to go with her
to pick up the pizzas. Thirty
minutes sufficed to hear
about her grandson and his husband
and their new jobs and their
house in escrow. A handsome
young Vermonter in Florida
visiting his dad. It's an anti-Santa
52 degrees and raining in the
Green Mountains. He's shaving
in the shower house, open
in the middle of the night like
a Kwik Trip. We could relieve
some holiday tension while
old folks Swanee-River-snore.
Share Manatees at Beth's Vero Beach
rental. The funniest mishearing

I ever met. Dylan's "Well
my sense of humanity has
gone down the drain," transcribed
as "Well my sensitive manatee
has gone down the drain."
Poor thing. And yet, an apt
image of man's out-crowding
of fellow beasts. Vero Beach Art
Museum. Talking with Beth's
Jeff in the gift shop, questioning
the value of colorful family tales.
His vaudevillian forebears on
their bikes. GREAT FEATS OF
BALANCING WHILE MOVING.
Bye-bye-embracing Beth in
the gravel driveway in the shade
of the old stable converted
to a studio for textile art.
Not used to the softness of
breasts against me. Memories
of dancing with Beth when we
were kids. Her association
of me with "Benny and the Jets."
Before I went for my Christmas
shower I thought about
the stars — every one of
them a Star of Bethlehem.
Every one, the herald of
a new child. Each child,
every Jesus there ever was,
lived, died and stayed dead.
Eventually their star dies too.
I was looking forward to

a clear view of this glittering
graveyard, thanking the little
water heater for pushing
me out the door so early
on the yuletide. But when
I got outside the sky was
eerily overcast and windy,
and I thought: *These are the
Christmas winds and this is how
the story ends*. There was another
man in the shower. I never saw
him but I heard him clearing
his throat as he was shaving.
A gentle constantly renewed
attempt to clear his throat.
It was the sound of a very
old man clearing his throat.
And then I thought: *How utter
is the transformation and
wouldn't it be wonderful
if Time's compassion left us with
a single faculty un-aged, even
if it's just the racket we make
when we clear our throat.*
Soon I was outside again,
surprised to see a clear sky.
Cellphone call in the middle
of lunch at the "Greek" joint.
The call no one knows what
to do with. So it gets passed
around like a birthday card
being signed at the office.
The ex-daughter-in-law no one

knows what to do with.
"Sounds like you have a cold."
"I'm fighting back tears."
Tears she doesn't
know what to do with —
or does she? How wrong
is it to suspect these are
strategic tears and her real
frustration is that the strategy
isn't working? The phone
as the intruder that soon
becomes indispensable,
like children I suppose.
I was promised mockingbirds
but they did not come.
If they did, they were unseen
and sadly dumb. I was told
they would sing the theme
songs of all their cousins.
Songs of nephews and nieces,
of which they have dozens.
I hoped that they would teach me
to steal other singers' songs.
I've been singing my own tunes
far, far, far too long. It was
threatened that mockingbirds
would recklessly divulge my
schemes. They would borrow
my varied voices to proclaim
my secret dreams. I waited for
them each morning, looked for
them on each street. Trailers lit
for Christmas. Small front yards,

stages for *tableaux vivants* —
actually, *plastiques* — some
secular, some that protest the
secular, some tacky, some
surprisingly self-possessed like
those blue-glowing fawns
foraging in night grass, so sweet-
looking one can't help
thinking they only want to
kiss the beetles and grubs.
They want to greet them
and shed gentle illumination
on their grassy books. It's not
going to work. I have to tap into
other-ly demented minds.
Dementia sufferers who lose
their ability to build a nest or put on
their shoes or conjure grandkids
on the phone to hear and impart
good news will tell you they have
not lost themselves. Ken is still
Ken. He just can't make this
plain with paper and pen. Jill
is still Jill though she's now more
likely to spill than to pour.
This loss of ability and retention
of identity is less true of states.
States, it seems, are very good
at losing themselves in Amazons
and Saharas of deceit.
The hallucinations of Alzheimer's
patients are entirely different
inasmuch as they are innocent.

When Granddad saw fires that
were not there, it was not for us
or for the nurses to beware.
When his cancer worsened and
his second son came to watch,
to keep him in the bed, to sleep
on the floor beside the bed; when
the pre-corpse rose naked in
the night to wrestle his son for
a belated blessing, it was not
for the son to say, "I'm no angel."
When Grandma lunched
with the senator at the Big Wheel,
why not inquire about the quality
of the meal? Oh, it may have
been poisoned but only with
the most innocent of poisons.
Really, you cannot make
too big a deal about the innocence
of Alzheimer's — or
the underhandedness
of states intentionally slipping
back into darkness, stupidly
dropping buckets full of
ambrosia into the dark of
a polluted well. Or the meanness
of laws that tie you to the mortgage
on a condo that jumped or was
cast into the pit through no
fault of yours. My parents
are in the lion's den. Will
Dad be Dan and muzzle
the lion's maw? Will Mom

be Daniella and remove the thorn
of paranoia from the lion's
paw? I see them, clear as an
innocent hallucination.
They are at the governor's press
conference. They raise their heads
like latches on gates, like lamps
on poles. They extend their long
necks like the Sandhill Cranes
whose necks are as long and straight
as a medieval herald's horn
when there were decrees to trumpet.
"For shame, Governor. There are
no schools (despite your detailed
claims) where the teachers
decided this girl shall become
a boy, that boy shall become a girl,
all in a whirlwind they deny to the
children's parents — or tell them
it's a tornado and they must take
cover. For Shame, Governor.
Either you know the truth and
are looking for goats to blame
or you are so lost in paranoia,
you will not believe anyone
when they tell you their name."
There he stands flanked by
his courtiers. How smoothly
he talks. I wish I could talk like
that at poetry readings at
public libraries that the governor,
not knowing true iniquity when
he sees it, calls dens of iniquity.

Dad, who's more pithy, adds:
"White chicks will peck
a brown chick to death. Aren't
you smarter than a chicken?"
The fan base for snuff films
is small. Maybe I'm wrong about
this. I know of the popularity
of public hangings and
gladiator combats. Still I think
most of us don't want
to see one snuff, much less 98.
The security footage from the condo
next to Champlain Tower South,
1:23 a.m. June 24th 2021,
looks like a postcard when
postcards were made
from paintings, not photographs —
looks like a colorized movie.
On the left, an ornamental plant
squirms. The water in the pool
is the tint of unhealthy jade. The pool
deck is about to kneecap the khaki
colored building. An enormous
cloud of dust goes up, and a whole
wing goes down, as though stepping
into a void. "Like it was
a planned implosion," an anchorman
observes. We've all seen those on
other news broadcasts. We've all
commented on the neatness, the
safety, speed, grace. But this
is not a clearing off of the old
to make way for the shiny.

This building isn't empty. This is
98 snuff films in an evening
gown. I knew an old swimming
pool that swallowed a condo stack.
No infinitive of purpose, but
mistakes abound. I knew
a hole in the ground that was
force-fed Babel. There were no
good outcomes from that treatment.
I know a writer who slid a tube
into his readers' thoughts
and poured in a truck-load of
disquieting shots of an ordinary
disaster. Round about that time
my parents and I saw "Rear Window"
in a restored movie house.
The men's lounge and its counter-
part were out of this world in
purple and wolf-gray plush,
with a pair of lobby round-seats
of crushed velvet. Grace Kelly
did something I've always wanted
to do: glide from lamp to lamp to lamp
in a dim room, answering *who are you?*
— one name at a time, switching
on the bulbs as I go. As for
James Stewart — the collision
of desperate cowardice and
useless love when Lisa is in
the killer's flat and the killer's
on his way up — is the best acting
Stewart ever did. I cast
another actor, probably Mike,

answering *who are you?* in my place.
Again the dim room, the arch
voice, each name shedding more
light on my face. But this time,
names I've never heard. True
names I've never heard.
"Sorry, I ain't gonna apologize,"
Old Dude said as he oozed down
I75 at ten miles per hour.
This was done and recorded
to suggest how long the
dark felt on the way to Uncle
Ray and Aunt Charlene's.
How long and how surrounded
by black and how huddled
(because cars make everyone
huddle). Two riders and one
driver who, medical crises
set aside, had never feared
for their lives. As close as
they'd come to the tautness
of soldiers on the eve of battle,
prisoners serving deadening
sentences, a family trying to
be mice while jackboots attack
the furniture below. Not very close,
I realize. But something ominous
made us feel the need for songs
and car games — and then
quashed songs and games.
How relaxed, the daytime
drive when dark that
could have hidden any horror

was replaced by miles and miles
of sugarcane. They were burning
here and there that day, but it
was a controlled, agricultural burn
and we were feeling too relieved
to think of funeral pyres or
Fahrenheit 451. When we
stopped to steal a stick of sugar
to take home to Mike, jungles,
Viet Cong and GIs were far
from our minds. Thinking only
gets you so far down or up I75.
Why steal sugarcane for Mike?
The look on his face when
he talks of sugarcane treats
he sucked at the Hanoi
Zoo when he was a big-headed
kid, could inspire me to high
crimes and misdemeanors.
After Patrick's funeral, the
mourners sat in Patrick's garage.
His collection of neon signs,
mounted on the walls, was
a spiritual reminder of beers
and bars and pool halls. The widow
was quiet, and we wondered
to what extent that was due
to her sickness. She had never
hesitated to criticize Patrick's
faux pas, and this step into
a neon dimension struck her
as the falsest of all his false
steps. After the reception,

we took down and boxed up
my parents' Christmas décor,
knowing we'd miss a sprig or
two, knowing in a week
she would come across a Santa
or a mini-wreath hanging around
like Jesus on the road to Emmaus —
hanging around like that or any other
story. After Susan's funeral,
they went straight home. Dad
worked in the wood shop and Mom
hemmed the pants it had taken him
hours to pick out. Later she
texted me that she was getting used
to the funerals. I knew this was
true and untrue. As usual,
she said nothing about her pending
collapse into the pool.

June 24

I get so excited about places where we sit
in domesticity, I can't sit still.
There's an unwanted thrill of Manifest Destiny.
Twelve stories of Champlain Tower South,
including a penthouse that wasn't
supposed to exist, defer to the weight
of a cloaked spaceship on the roof.
A tornado makes a rare appearance
in the Czech Republic, choosing village over city.

June 25

Search and Rescue
and other Proustian missions.
On the gray sofa, Mike's heel
fits my curved palm like a blackjack.
18 Chinese teenagers
die in a fire while practicing
Martial Arts. 16 more are injured.
They chose the wrong Art.
Martial versus Marital.
Marital in league with Martial.
I'm on the lookout
for meaning in an extra letter
or a reversal. Plan. Plant. Planet

June 26
The Delta Variant reigns
from Tallahassee to Key West.
A chronic Robert Johnson
fan, I wish I was talking
about his Delta Blues. Wish they
were so much a part of me,
my shoes could play them
on their shoestrings even
when they're untied. Or
when I step on them. I
carry my vaccination card in
my wallet, wishing
someone would ask to see it.
Like there's a club I could
get into that would make
a difference. A club
guaranteed not to be
Pulse but to always have a
pulse. Someone who would
show me his card which
would turn out to be
identical to mine.

June 27
Something has changed with
this 78 player — or with this 78
record — such that Rosemary
Clooney sounds half woman,
half man — and under water.
The death count in Surfside
is nine. "Mambo Italiano."
This record was made before
Billy Strayhorn produced
Clooney and got Duke's band
to back her. She was considered
a novelty singer. On the red sofa
Mike reads the instructions for
the home test while the swab
in my nose brings on tears,
for want of a better word.

June 28
I can't believe you're still trying to be wise.
I've got your wise crap
coming out my eyes. Ukraine and NATO
dance in the Black Sea, arousing
the jealousy of Ukraine's former lover.

Tim to Mike:
The anchor-people keep saying
the residents were sleeping
at the time of the collapse.
This is why we need artists.
Mike to Tim:
I take your point. But it doesn't take
an artist to speculate on the worlds
that unfold at one in the morning
behind closed condos.
Tim to Mike:
I take your point.
I should have said art, not artists.

June 29

House Resolution 3005 removes
Confederate monuments from
Federal sites. I'd love to be alive
in 3005 and find all
such monuments — stone, bronze
or mental — gone. When
does Search and Rescue
turn to Recovery? If you're
talking about the bodies artists
seek, is there a difference?
And when you say 'recovery'
does the possibility of the
dead getting better
flare in your speech centers?
On the beige sofa the migration
to Florida is starting: Mike's
44-year-old elbow is as touchy
as a real old lady who swallowed
a real bug.

June 30
Mom and I play with our ice cream
cones. All people I haven't known insist
on their privacy. My parents hint at
my inheritance because I made a snide
remark about the affluent neighborhood
we drove through to get to this McDonalds.
("Lock the car doors. This is a sketchy
part of town.") One thing
is sure: My folks won't wind
up in a Florida aquifer.

Three days after Barb's funeral:
Mom dropped by Barb's double-
wide to check on the new widower
and to rescue the Christmas cacti,
one of them as pink as a girl's
or — before the colors were
switched — a boy's baby
blanket. Brandy was still around,
planning to stay with her dad for
the rest of the week, to breathe as
much Florida February as her lungs
could reap before flying back
to New Haven. They sat deep in or
on the edge of their seats and rehashed
the letters from Barb to her daughters,
opened and read at the service —
each like the girls' memories of
watching from a vacation backseat
their parents do the Watusi on

the shoulder of the road to a loud
thin song from the radio. Brandy
went to the kitchen for iced tea
and came back with a gecko.
She sat with her legs crossed,
her hand on her knee, the gecko
on the bassinet of her palm, its
belly turned up for her caressing
index. Brandy and her dad
talked about people we'd never
heard of. (How did I get there and
why did no one comment on my
impossible presence?) We were
quiet then. Time was measured by
the gecko's rising heat. Mom said,
"Brandy you're an animal
whisper," and Brandy went outside
and laid the gecko in a bush.
"Brandy," I sang, "You're a fine girl,
what a good life you would be."
My mom misspeaks and I mishear,
each with surprising meaning.
Brandy didn't know the song,
and I thought: *I'd like Mom's life;*
she goes to so many funerals
and I to so few. We are quiet for
another degree or two. Then I say,
"According to one theory blue
was the Virgin's and pink was
a weaker form of Mars, the red
planet and God of Open-Carry
Bars." Someone, maybe Barb,
asked with surprise, "Where did

you come from?" I won't keep
my lips pure. I can't find
what I wrote on the bus.
I remember it was dark, then it
was dim, then it was light.
It was not during the 2021
ride, my first trip of the Pan-
demic, when I expected
all the passengers to be masked.
(Only I was.) I remember
a vision of the land between
home and the airport as it was
before Europeans came.
The differences between that
road and I75 were illusory,
but that doesn't mean they
weren't important, does it?
Cane fields flank the banks of I75.
At distant points, east and west,
smoke goes up. The sacrificed
beast is best. Incriminating
documents are being burned.
All my books are burning —
not to suppress their ideas, but
because they weigh me down
as I move from town to town.
My records are melting. Not
because the Beatles were
too hot for their tight leather
breeches. The clothes I wore
when I was sowing wild rice
are burning. Many of the shirts
could be mistaken for flaming

butterflies. These cane bonfires
burn in solidarity with forest fires
that are becoming as normal
as mass shootings. Maybe
they are forest fires in their
own right. Maybe all
flammable flora conspires
against us. At last a conspiracy
theory I can sink my teeth into.
Predominant images of Dad
are like this: He's seventy
and stretched from fingertip
to toe-tip, half in the upstairs
bedroom, half out the window,
drilling a screw into the roof
to keep the air conditioner
from turning Kamikaze.
I'm helping him guide a plank
across the table saw, and I
picture myself in the plank's place
and think: *That isn't apt.*
But maybe my brother
would say it was aptness itself.
This morning I see our father
in a new twilight,
moon and planets in a typical
Floridadmixture. He walks
softly from room to room
checking our sleep, making
sure our joints are tight,
making sure we and the doors
are locked and door-chained.
He is Florence Nightingale.

Having drunk his nightly
nighting ale, he yawns.
On wordy I75 it's every bladder
for itself. The rest stop signs
have been kidnapped
or the rest stops trapped
underground. Whichever,
there are none to be found.
But you say those are smoke
signals telling us where to
reconvene after the war, telling
us what to bring and what to
forsake, telling us how precious
we'll be when finally the weather
really does break. The sky
says we've all got it wrong.
The cane isn't on fire. Those
are not smoke columns. Those
are publicity stunts, propaganda
from activists who were
always too solemn for my
taste. I look out the window.
Like sound rising to join meaning,
smoke accosts clouds. Both
are random Manifestations of Beauty.
I look out the window. An
ambulance passes. Then I
notice *Animal Rescue* tattooed
on metal, a thing I haven't seen
in any other state. Looking out
the window is an ultra-simple
act. What lies beyond the window
is complexity itself. This

moment's window reveals far
too many stagecoaches in the sky.
I look out the window and see
past generations bound for
Disney World, and wonder how
many future generations will
make the trek. D. W.. No, not
Griffith, maker of "Birth of a
Nation" and — incongruously —
"Intolerance," bearing in mind
that humans are essentially
incongruous. No, I'm talking
about Disney World, the Grand-
daddy enclave, the Magic Kingdom
within the Tragic Kingdom.
Founded on the first of October,
Mike's birthday, seven years
before he was born in Hanoi —
blue in the face, much to
his grandmother's consternation,
blue as Krishna, I've always said,
and now add: blue as the Genie
voiced by Robin Williams.
At the time of writing, 77,000
employees and over 25,000 acres.
I do a lot of reading, trying
to understand Disney's
relationship with Queer
World. The problem is 'Disney'
is thousands of people and
jungle-big tangles of film and
decades of conflicting pressures.
In the end, all I can say is:

It started as bad as Anita Bryant
and now it's fighting with the
governor — fighting for the
sake of Queer Respect. On
the backroad to Aldi, I look
out the window at habitations
that make my dad shudder.
I find them alluring with their shadowy
hanging moss on cypress and oak,
greasy gravel and half-pirate,
half-witch houses that breathe
with everything else. I look
out the window and see Jafar and
Rick Scott in a kiss Disney
suppressed despite its support
for their couple-dom. I see
transparencies of the many
places Mike and I have lived
where nary a torch-bearing mob
marched on us. Among our bright
differences: Mike grows tired
of places. I grow to love them
(also, he social-distances with
humming microwave ovens).
I look out the window and see
a collection of old postcards,
the kind based on paintings, not
photos, of the Seven Mile
Bridge, which I'd love to see
from a distance. It's beautiful
but I have gephyrophobia. No,
Dad's not as pretty as he was
when he lived in a crummy

house in a village he loves
to recollect. And yet, how much
of himself, his time, money
and inflexibility he has spent
on maintaining nice houses
where all things are tucked
away when they're not in use,
as though he expects
a surprise visit from
House & Garden any
minute now. He is beautiful
turning a bowl on a lathe,
carving a boat the size of
a red wagon and a captain
taller than the mast to stand
fast beside it. These effigies
on the front lawn declare:
77 years we lived far inland.
Now we join the Sunshine
State of hurricanes and salt air.
Excuse me while I comb my
thick black hair. From the bow
of the toy boat I spy the year
I was diagnosed and Mike
thought my parents should
have stayed up North. I see
the Christmas I didn't fly
'cause COVID was everywhere:
east. west. north, south. The year
the family's politics split
infinitives definitively.
Uncles, aunts and cousins
chose to boldly go where Trump

and anti-science not so
much led as dumped them.
My mom, who was never
passionate about any
candidate, discovered vehemence
in her dislike for the Donald,
The Cry Baby in Chief,
and all that he stood — or
rather, slouched for. Yet
this divided house stood.
For Mom and Dad,
familial love trumps
political disgust. And they
would rather swallow live
bait than take on
un-needful conflict. Now
it's the summer of 2022
and Uncle and Aunt
moved permanently from
Indiana to CP1 a month ago.
What with painting
their new house and fixing
up Uncle's wood shop,
and playing pegs and jokers,
they are a Harmonious Unit.
I'm talking on my flip-top,
feeling ashamed of my
new stammer, looking out
the window at a walled lot
full of vacant RVs. They call it
the Bullpen. I'm walking on
the solid black water that
divides two regiments of

palm trees, going slow,
imitating golf carts that
will lumber out from under
carports in a few hours.
I sag on aluminum bleachers
observing the ways 16 elder
shufflers don't let their sticks
touch what they shouldn't.
The British chap measures his
movements like Mary Poppins,
pushing the stick to its umbrella
length then drawing it back with
girlish relish. Canada Jenny
feigns acute vapors and asks
me to take her place, a gambit
in the old people's campaign
to drag me into the game. In
the shower I wash off the stink
 of shuffling. I enjoy my curves
and calves and my flat hand
like a knife in a warm loaf.
I kill the water, yank back the
curtain, look into the mirror as
though I've walked in on someone.
At two in the morning I
climb into the Bullpen for
exploration I've neglected
for decades. I move as catlike
as I can among commodious
graves that would make most dead
folk salivate. I am a spy
from the Army of the Living sent
to gather intelligence. I creep

toward voices. I recognize Mary
Poppins' tone but not the deep
West Virginian drawl that surrounds
it like warm arms. The voices
speculate. What will the West
Virginian's niece exclaim
when she opens her gift?
Mastering the urge to whistle
"The Bridge On the River Kwai,"
I belly-crawl under a Winnebago.
Tomorrow I'll tell Mike I saw a
bull and his mate in the pen.
They reminded me of Civil War
soldiers in daguerreotypes —
only they had half shed
their uniforms. Dad dropped
another hint today. The house
on the golf course could come
to Mike and me in due course.
Which neither of us wants.
This project is set up in such a way
that it must end when my
contact with Florida ends.
Which feels sinister, like
I'm a gator with a clock in my
gut, treading smelly water till the
grand finale, my parents' death.
Aquifers spoil smell- taste.
Brushing my teeth, washing
my face cease to be purifying
acts. Sex and even love can
cash in on the same ambiguity.
What is an aquifer? Any formation

that holds or guides ground-
water for wells, springs, spring-
breaks, holidays, a character
and all his mistakes. It's the
sulfates in the aquifers — so
what are they? Salts or esters of
sulfuric acid. Ester: a compound
made when acid and alcohol
react, eliminating a water molecule.
Grandma in her bedridden
hallucinations became an
eliminating witch.
She conjured a mistress for
my dad: the old woman
in the next room, who made
noises like a patrol car parked
on the shoulder of a road,
no one to chase, no one to entrap,
no one to rush to the ER. Still
she wailed. Grandma eliminated
her with the unwitting
connivance of the nurse trying
 to eliminate Grandma. Granddad
also told a lie of elimination, saying
my brother was plotting to
eliminate me — but he (Granddad)
foiled the plot, wrestled my
brother to the mat and
denounced him to the Secret
Police. I think Granddad, in spite
of his faith and his stubbornness,
felt bad about trying to eliminate a
movement in me, one so innate,

he saw it as soon as I started to walk.
On Ixora Street a tree speaks.
I've just arrived from northern
Europe. The palm trees look
monstrous. Surely they're a
species I know, altered by the
advanced stage of a disease I
don't know. I note how it kills
branches, blanches trunks and beats
leaves into blades. I name it
after myself as though bringing
fresh sickness were an honorable
act. When I learn my mistake I give
the bush a Latin name and think
I've done a grand thing.
Setting aside my reluctance
to strategize about family
(I'm dreamy enough
to think families shouldn't
be governed by our Cesars)
I walk my dogged perplexity
up and down predawn Ixora
Lane. The solution I seek
is blocked by thoughts like:
My parents are happy not
knowing the pronunciation
of the street they live on,
happily don't wonder for
74 years of "The First Noel"
what Noel means,
feel worldly looking at
their neighbors' American,
Canadian and British flags

without ever thinking: English-
Speaking. Two hours later
the palms silhouetted against
a pink-blue wash approach
the historicity of Christmas cards
set in the Holy Land.
If "No ideas but in things" goes
for battle plans, my options
are overwhelmingly at hand.
A tropical evergreen planted
guard-like at the gate
raises rich pink pompoms
eager to sit atop my cap.
When the locals fail to master
its name, it becomes
West Indian Jasmine.
It starts the tour my mother
gives my new sister-in-law.
The flora and fauna of this
village-sized Florida park.
Year-long blooming Blue
Daze, Bougainvillea, Hibiscus.
Burr-studded grasses. Virginia Tom,
who prints my boarding
passes. His wife Mary who
thinks I'm a hoot. Canadian
Tom and Mary, who adopted
a cutting of a wandering Jew my
brother brought home from
Summer Bible school camp
when he was nine. They
watered it into a green-purple
mane worthy of Samson.

Strategy in objects? None
will convert this holiday visit
into a lifetime. America won't
be folded up like a Monopoly
board, tumbling the L.A. boot
and the Boston thimble into
the fold. If we all end up in
the same hard red retirement
home, it will be too late.
About the demented and the
dementing. I will dark-word
them to death, bright-word
them to life, deck them from
tiptop to toe with Floridadjectives
and Floridadverbs. You,
I will strange-word to distraction
and the fun you have will be
a fraction of the fun I give.
(From the name, a trans singer
springs. West Indian Jasmine
in a midnight blue, midnight green,
midnight red patola — but no,
only when she retreats into the bed-
room of my mind does she dress thus.
On my mind's stage or in its
Pulse she dances in strangling
jeans and viny silk blouses.)
Dad would have none of it
when Granddad tried to convince
him to beat me into the shape
and hardness of a proper boy.
They fought and didn't speak
for over a year. Most of my

life I was told an edited version.
It was all about toy guns.
All about Saigon and Hanoi
and Walter Cronkite and young
arrivals to the East and West
and old, old forces determined
to destroy. I was 55 when Mom
told me. The issue was how
her in-laws treated me and urged
her to treat me. Orange trees, join
Orange trees, play footsie.
If your oranges taste bland,
who will call you Tootsie?
"Verde, que te quiero, Verde,"
Lorca cried. But not oranges.
They want to be green's
complement in and outside.
From 1902 to 1998, from China
to Palm Beach County, Citrus
Greening leapt on tiny wings
bringing life to some, death to
others — and shrunken profits
like balls in a cold swimming pool.
A knife in his right hand, a runty
green orange in his left —
five generations guide the swift,
deft movement of blade
through fruit. Then a quick
squeeze shows that the ball
still squirts before the two
halves are dropped to orchard
dirt. The taste is a tad less sweet
than what we're used to, but

when the juice is blended with
juice from healthy trees it's
acceptable. The trouble
is, when you play hide-and-seek,
the canopies don't conceal you.
Still it's grand, the way the farmer
cuts and talks and has no
intention of giving up. Grand
to see the scientists deploy
 short-term defenses while
searching for the über-tree that
will plump the groves back to their
former denseness. A kind of
hide-and-seek with bugs
whose eyes are easy to fool.
Swaddling clothes that give
the saplings a fighting chance.
Grand the workers in T-shirts,
jeans and boots made of earth,
striding the fields with spades
and water tanks that lumber like
beasts. What if Citrus Greening
should win? That would be grand
too. And perhaps it would teach
us to stop dubbing this or that *grand*.
Orange, how I want you, Orange.
Gaze at your navel. The grove'll
not be as pretty as it was fifteen
years ago. For now, it is beautiful
like the Madwoman of Chaillot
flapping her gauzy scarves and
dusty boa. Green, how I want you
as I look out the window

at the concrete of utter un-greenness.
Long hours between naps and
CD compilations. Mom texts
in the back and Dad powers
through, barely stopping to eat
on the way to Miami, where
I do my best to channel my brother.
In a former life I was a general
who disliked but could stomach
the gruesome. In my memoirs
I coined the phrase: You win
some; you lose some. The
book won me more respect
than any battlefield ever did.
In a former life I was the
quintessential soldier about
whom the enemies of War
wrote: He was just a kid. In
a former life I was a surveyor.
Previously, I was a bricklayer
who had been in legendary days
a fearsome dragon slayer.
In this life I have a brother
who puts rhymes in my mouth.
We used to go places together.
I drove and he looked out the
window. Sometimes he resented
my control. Sometimes I
resented his leisure. But
we both knew it was meant
thus for the brief time
we went places together. (I hope
he makes it clear: elimination

was Granddad's fantasy, not mine.)
I'll be up at 3:00 in the
morning, at peace, at my desk.
He lived at the southern end
of I75 for three years. Year One,
he was newly divorced, had a
new fiancée lagging in California.
That Christmas, for the first time
in decades, maybe the last time,
the calendar convened the four of us,
the nuclear family, the original
Broadway cast. Year Two,
the new woman joined us.
It was the honeymoon period
for her and our parents.
They bonded over baby pictures
while he sulked (strove to
concentrate) in his vast chair.
Year Three, the Pandemic was
nine months old, eight more
than Zuzu. No vaccine yet,
I stayed in Wisconsin.
My parents were ushered into
the baby's presence under
strict supervision. When I met
her, a year later, she was taking steps,
happily falling on her tush
in North Carolina in a patrician
house the dogs and cats
shook like a bush or a shoe.
The reincarnated surveyor/
bricklayer/dragon slayer had
become again the great gainsayer.

I75 hugs the border between
Ohio and Indiana. On its way to
the militias of the Upper Peninsula,
it passes Ann Arbor, which Mike
and I vacated in 2011. Shortly before
Brother and family moved to NC,
Uncle Ray died and Charlene
went to live with her gay grand-
son in Texas. Things that I love
when they're gone. I75 is now one.
The people that helped. Plus
one dog. Eighty rescue units,
Miami-Dade Fire Rescue
Aerial 19, FEMA, Urban Search
and Rescue Florida Task Forces
1 and 2, Ambulances from
Hatzalah of South Florida,
Ohio, Virginia, Israel, The Israel
Defense Force's Home Front
Command Search and Rescue Team,
trauma counselors from United
Hatzalah, The Miami Heat,
World Central Kitchen, Direct
Relief, The American Red Cross,
Mexico, Escambia County,
The United States Army Corps
of Engineers, ZAKA, Cadena
International, The Miami Marlins.
People fell from the US, Paraguay,
Argentina, Canada, Cuba,
Venezuela, Colombia, Uruguay,
Australia, Brazil, Costa Rica, Italy,
the United Kingdom and

the Animal Kingdom. Also
there was one Fire Spirit —
maybe the flame of the Burning
Bush? Talking to whom? Urging what?
I keep wondering if the dog
met the resident cat that survived.
(Its family did not.) If
HELP ME were scratched, carved,
crayoned, sprayed on every wall
you looked at (it is) you would
go mad. "Look at the high-rise.
Can you tell the structure
from the ornament?"
"No, I can't." "Is that good?"
"It depends. Is the structure
masquerading as ornament?
Or is it the other way round?"
On the first day a voice was heard
till 11:00 a.m.. The voice
of the ruins from the ruins.
It was a woman's voice.
It was Woman's voice. It reminded
me of Yoko Ono and Kate
Smith and Beyonce.
What did the ruins say?
The simplest thing that can be said.
The incarnate spirit of
monotony. A team of true
humanitarians was inspired
by a throbbing more urgent than art.
They strove to release
that voice as writers and
singers strive to find theirs.

Like a brother or sister
deaf from birth. Is there a witness
whose superior ears will hear
the voice now that it's gone?
The voice of the collapse didn't
last long. The woman's voice showed
more stamina. According to received
family law, my mother had
the voice of the changeless till
she exposed the sill and it blew away.
My voice — actually my words —
are beginning to slur. It won't
be long before my speech is as
worn as Joe Biden's. And there were
among the rescuers, volunteers
attending to the rescuers' wellbeing.
They fed them and gave them water.
They monitored their health
and state of mind. They wiped
sweat from their eyes. They
cooled their feet. They spoke words
of praise and encouragement
like Athena and Mercury
in *The Odyssey*. They succored
them and would not suffer them
to work while the hidden fire
put forth its choking smoke.
Nor would they allow them
near the un-fallen tower. For their
sakes, they brought that tower down
as gingerly as the Nazarene's friends
deposed the Nazarene. When the
rescuers attempted to work

beyond their endurance, the helpers
made them lie down. These
human-sent angel facsimiles were
inevitable, for in disaster they and
opportunists arise. When a building
takes its own life, there is much
soul-searching and recrimination
among those who knew the
building and those who did not.
Was it suicide or an overdose?
Weren't red flags whipped?
Were onlookers blind to them?
Did they see and ignore? Adjacent
buildings turn to each other
and quietly ask, "Have you ever
considered self-demolition?"
Some answer truthfully. Some lie.
In the clubhouse the organ plays
its automatic drums.
On December 23rd the choir
from a local middle school
comes. The accompaniment,
mostly from a machine,
gives these tweens and teens
a semi-professional sheen.
In the chair where Jessie, who
always wore a flamboyant
hat, sits, a hat that doesn't
flame at all now rises. Donna,
the boisterous Canadian, says
her last words were, "Time to
call it quits." I sit in on
Mom's exercise hour. Much

of the work is done from a
sitting position. Even
sitting down, I'm alarmed
by a loss of power I hadn't
noticed. There's a meeting
at which Dad reads the
financial report and a pasta
dinner for residents and out-
siders to raise money to
repair the shuffleboard courts.
One night all the men,
including my dad, are in
drag for fun — something I've
never done — more fun,
it looks like, than drag shows
I've seen. The ride to the
club on a golf cart at night
is swift and bumpy.
The cool air, if you've been here
for as little as two weeks,
is cold. It's about the human
mind, not about turning old.
In the aftermath of the shooting
at Pulse, I get lots of sympathy,
especially from women.
I show Marilyn, who was an
English teacher, the following poem.
The lights, the drum sounds
that pulse in discotheques
everywhere, if only they
could set bounds of
impenetrable defense. But
had the lights been

brighter and not fitful,
they would not have stopped
the event; they would only
have lit the horror of dark, hard
pulses sent to stop
49 living drums.
The infernal atmosphere
of such clubs,
let it pause for a time.
Do not let this Death Dance
stand. Out of the
many, I see mother and son
sharing a face: round
smiles and beaver incisors;
 sharing a name: Christine
and Christopher —
Christ-follower and
Christ-bearer. I scour the
web for his friends' names.
Their anonymity becomes
their beauty as they flank
their slain friend's mother,
rubbing her arms as
though the grief is in her
triceps — as she once rubbed
dirt from her son's cheek.
Their dark lashes would fan
her if they had the power.
Moses and Elijah,
they rise from the
convention floor. Good news
lights up the Teleprompter.
I make them a dance

company of two writhing
on a stage where the female
vocalist struts. The son's
final choreographic gift:
letting his mom carry him
up the street to the trauma center.
How willing the body seems
when the will has left it.
An hour in the Florida room,
alone before dawn. The golf
course is a freshly shorn grave-
yard. Headphones in perfect
unison read aloud choruses of
"Mexico City Blues". A vast
chunk of the world in my Mac-
book's memory banks (8 GB).
I'm surprised but not perplexed
by this news: Red Foley is the
perfect chaser to a whiskey
shot of Kerouac. Bongos! Yes,
those are bongos driving
"Don't Let the Stars Get
in your Eyes" relentlessly
forward. Red Foley's mellow
manly voice wears Kerouac's
"Go to Hell Cap"
Go to Hell.
Go to Heaven.
Two weeks in Florida.
All are ways of saying we'll meet
nowhere when we're nothing
again although we never
ceased to be beautifully nothing.

The next song is
"That Little Boy of Mine."
This is how my tone deaf Dad
wishes he sounded. And
that's God the Father and
Momotaro's adoptive papa
thinking of toddler Jesus
and toddler me and Momotaro
already stronger than any
toddler since Hercules.
We all thank Nashville that Country
Music isn't embarrassed by our
shared sentimentality. I cry and
hear my Mom's deteriorating
language skills (she says
chinnylinnal for *sentimental*).
I hear my own misshapen
words. I feel the deterioration
inherited from her x bone stirring
in me, nudging us toward mutual
incomprehensibility — or to
a private language. Maybe they're
the same thing. The first cries.
The chorus of cries set off
when the conductor gave that
awful protracted downbeat.
Cries heard by fellow choristers,
by neighbors fleeing down the
stairs and the first of the first
responders. Later the solitary
cry, the solo, the aria desperate
for air. Then the silence. Cries
from the pandemic of loneliness.

Then the silence of souls
resigned to isolation. Desantis:
"You do not have to wear those
masks. I mean, please take
them off. Honestly, it's
not doing anything, and we've
got to stop this COVD theater,
so if you want to wear it, fine,
but this is ridiculous." To
young people standing behind
him at an indoor press conference.
The students, embarrassed, remove
their protection as the touchy
governor turns from them to
the podium in a huff. Me to
Desantis: "You might as well doff
your political mask. We can
see through it." Me to all
continents that are not safe
out of the closet: "You are not
your mask. Before us lies
a great task." I lie on the
floor with my eyes closed and
begin to be points of contact
(knee to carpet, jawline to
cushion, hand to cheek). Awareness
of these points and the thing that is
aware — I have them.
A rescue team was sent to find
a rescue team that was sent to
find a rescue team. How many
layers till we contemplate the lot
of people trapped in rubble,

the lot of prisoners in solitary,
the lot of prison guards, the lot
of first responders. Like the
swallowed and swallowing beasts,
the iterations go on. There's nothing
necessarily death-imposing about
a horse. The lyrics affirm the certainty
of Death and the un-solvability of
 the mystery of identity. Eventually
why? collides with *I don't know.*
At some point the Earth evolves
into a Venus Human Trap. At no point
do parents understand: Loving
the kids equally doesn't mean
liking them the same and all this
cumulative tale of liking
is the thing that tames. At some
point we all get lost in our clothes.
At some point we boil in the mid-
night oil we burned.

July 1
News from the Art World. Indigenous
protesters toppled a statue of Queen
Victoria in Winnipeg. I wonder how
the old girl felt, rocking back and
forth, back and forth before
pitching face first to the ground —
maybe into the arms of Saddam
Hussein. Lesbian delights
were never outlawed in the U.K..
Victoria dismissed the idea that
women would do such things.

July 2
The connotation of *break through*
takes a dark turn as break-through
infections become commoner and
commoner. The "cobwebs" in
Mom's vision are impervious
to the ophthalmologist's charms.
Warping in the middle of this
Guy Lombardo 78 makes the
uncredited male vocalist
sound like a whistle-blower
or kidnapper using a voice disguiser.
Any such warping in this document?

July 3
This is to accuse you. This is
to accuse me. This is to
pardon us both. This is to
wonder, in the small and vast
senses of the verb. Why are my
parents' friends dead-set
on my playing their games?
In Italy, the collapse of a serac
killed seven and injured thirteen.
I know about seracs because
a geologist once hurt me in bed.

July 4
Florida is not my home.
I am a carpet bagger/bugger.
The changes I bring
are well known.
The changes bagging
will work on me
are yet to be felt. In Iraq
several hundred people
breathe chlorine gas
and look it in the eye
to the detriment of lungs
and corneas. In India
a bus goes face-first
into a gorge, killing sixteen
passengers.

July 5
26 of the people
kidnapped by bandits at a
boarding school in Nigeria
are rescued by the army.
In Georgia (the European
one) the offices of the
organizers of a Pride parade
are broken into and trashed.
I watch the 2014 film *Pride,*
which always makes me bawl
at the end when coal miners
in glorious buses roll in.

July 6
Workers break into
previously unaccessible
rooms of the rubble of
Champlain Tower. Rooms
no one wants to enter, where
hope grows quiet. I'm
wintering on the sofa, trying
to pay attention to Rachel
Maddow. Distracted by a sound
outside I can't identify.
Neither the sound nor the outside.

July 7
It has many names,
all ways of avoiding the name
Love. The name on its
immigration papers
is more a transliteration
than a translation.
Free vaccines in the US
should be the happiest news
story of the year.

July 8
The ground is saturated
with verse. The words that make
up the verse are dissolved like
nutrients in water. An ideas
man, Mike waits for vast
acres of mirrors and an
irrigation system on the
scale of the Interstate.

July 9
43 people still hide
in Champlain's hide-and-seek,
one of the worst games in
the country's history. China
moves the giant panda from
endangered to *vulnerable*.
It's unclear how the giant
panda rates China — or
homo sapiens. The brain's
not moving fast enough
to know which chord/card to
play today today today — a way
of stalling till tomorrow.

July 10
Robert E. Lee and
Stonewall Jackson — well,
their bronze imitators anyway —
finally outstayed their
welcome in Charlottesville.
Oops, you see what happened
there? Looking for a fresh
way to phrase their removal,
I accidentally hid the fact
that many Virginians are
angry to see them go.

July 11
Death toll, 90.
Missing, 31. The media
(that's us) focus on the
numbers. They're not
comforting, but they're
steadying. A way to
manage the story so
it's not as impactful
as the collapse that started
everything.

July 12
My parents are with us
in Wisconsin. Mike says,
"No need to go and get, go
and get like you guys usually
do. Stay put and talk about stuff."
We take a picture — four
of us on the sofa kind of like
a Christmas card. I can't wait
to show it to my students.

July 13
Dad says, "This
country's not ready to
elect a woman president."
Mom says the country's
full of people who are out and
out racist. They also say
Mike and I have lots of allies.
Numbers like they
never imagined when
I came out to them
(not really the right
term, considering they
already knew) at the age
of 22. That feels right.
It feels like the majority
of Americans are
all right with us. It
feels like we don't have
to worry as long as we stay
here. Within a year it
will be clear that rule
by a rightwing
minority is not
unthinkable.

July 14

The thing about
cranes is not that they're
better than us. It's just
that there's much, much
less riding on them.
Bastille Day and I'm
feeling very "Best of times,
worst of times."
Could sure use a
Dickensian coincidence
to go our way. A sleeping
seismograph.

July 15

Who can comprehend the
judgment of man's hand?
In Europe from the U.K.
to Turkey, Rain and River
collaborate to clarify
and enumerate. 243
people dead. Twelve
billion dollars drowned.
I wish you had come to me
context-free. Potential is
rapidly being filled in.
If this neighborhood were
the sky, soon there'd be no
room for the sun.

July 16
If I were actually sleeping,
my amiability would peel itself
from me like the decal of a
boy's name on my 10th
grade notebook or the size
strip (extra small)
on the American Eagle jeans
I gave Mike for Christmas.

July 17
At Surfside authorities
have identified
95 to 97 victims for 95 to 97
otherworld grooms or brides;
a handful of friendships that tested
true like a well wrought
handgun; the same amount
of friendships that tested like
those guns after they were
softened by the sun;
a ton of broken temple stones
that — if stone were like
air (we've all breathed some
that Napoleon breathed)
could be among the stones
Samson used to grind
his tormentors' bones.

July 18
Senior survivors have moved back home
like millennial college grads. Or they've
moved into shelters — physical and
mental — they scorned.

July 19
The very first responder
is dreaming. The footage from
his body cam has been seen by
more people than you can
shake a bad conscience at.
Some have seen it more times
than I've seen *The African Queen*.
It's an unseemly way to become
a cinematographer. In the dream
he's skiing. It's night and he
has only a flashlight to guide him.
He realizes the flakes
caught with their pants down
in his flashlight beam
are dust, not snow. He wakes
and becomes upright like the
infamous security footage
played in reverse.

July 20
I say to Mike, "Two
buildings went up that night.
The building of dust stressed the
ephemeral. It was a fleeting high-rise
that entered lungs and eyes.
It could be — it was tasted.
It was stage makeup for a stage
crew forced into acting.
Solid stuff pretending to be spirit,
it couldn't be trusted. The second
 stuff was solid but bigger and
unashamed of its solidity. It resembled
a hill more than a building."

July 21
UNESCO says The Liverpool Maritime
Mercantile City is so altered
it can no longer be a World Heritage Site.

July 22
Yahweh denies involvement
in Surfside Collapse —- tells
reporters, "This was not Jericho."
I've heard no one ascribe
the catastrophe to him and suspect
the comment stems from a desire
to remain or seem to remain relevant.

July 23
The Rescue and Recovery mission officially ends.

July 26
The final victim is identified.
The sounds of cameras being
packed up seem to pronounce
the nam. Clicks a bit
inarticulate, but more definitive
than words. Mike and I discuss
the pro forma declarations that
accompany every public tragedy.

June 24 - July 26
More disasters than you can imagine
were barely averted. More than all the sparks
from all the fireworks that lit and colored
faces in Disney World and Disney Land —
times God knows how many fingers.

drip drip drip
One guy went to the Seminole
Casino in Tampa
and bet a small fortune
on his fury.
drip drip drip
The president of a play
for pay scheme
cut his fury out with
a cheese cutter.
drip drip drip
A woman determined
to be a true Christian
if it killed her
gave everything she had
to a crooked church,
the only kind that would
take it.
drip drip drip
There was a leaky
homeless kid.
All of her — the essence
and the incidental —
leaked onto the steps
of the Jacksonville
Public Library.
drip drip drip
The aquifers forgive
everything,
sin or no sin.
drip drip drip

Gentle rain completely
eroded Heaven, Hell
and Purgatory
but the earth remains.
drip drip drip
A professional Sit-down
Hydrofoiler slew the Hydra.
drip drip drip
Six dogs —
not a pack, they
just happened to have
the same dog-walker —
hallucinated they were
sled dogs and dragged
the walker for three blocks
causing serious injury.
drip drip drip
The same six dogs
dedicated the rest of their
dog years to rescuing
children and old people
and now and then
a high-as-a-kite surfer.
drip drip drip
There's a sect in Fort Myers
that believes
our personalities
accumulate
in a celestial bucket
a drop at a time
and when the bucket
overflows
it spills into this world

and that is birth.
drip drip drip
You've got some light
on your face.
It looks like sunlight.
"Get it off!
Get it off of me!"
drip drip drip
The Saint Johns River
is a great place
for a birthday party.
I've gone there every year
since I was 21 — and oh
the fun! You can't
imagine the fun!
splash splash splash
There was a horse
who regurgitated a cow
who threw up a goat
who vomited a dog
who spit up a cat
who coughed up a bird
who spewed a spider
who expectorated a fly
who released an old lady.
She was a mess, of course,
but thrilled to be free
of every creature
from the fly to the horse.
wish wish wish
One Gus says the sun
is not the breeze.
Opposite Gus says the sun

is the breeze.
What happens next
depends on how they feel
about each other.
churn churn churn
goes the wash cycle
in the laundry room at
CP1. Paula, who teaches
Gospel Crafts in her trailer
twice a week greets me,
smiles, starts a load,
sits down and after
a few niceties says she
wants to talk about Salvation.
She's utterly flummoxed
when I close my book
and say. "Good. I want
to talk about that too.
I'm sure I can give you
some good advice."
cough cough cough
Death doesn't wear a black
hood and robe. He
doesn't knock. He
appears in the La-Z-Boy
crumpled like Granddad
in his crumpled suit
quiet as a crumpled
handkerchief
but furious at his sons
for not forcing him to seek
the treatment he refused.
What is the sound of one

paddle paddled
in crystal green water
gently by a gentle man
so as not to alarm
the gentle aquatic
elephants of Blue Spring?
that sound that sound that sound
The manatee counter
moves as slowly
as the manatees
speaking to friends
he's seen for years —
"By their scars shall ye
know them." "Everything
is clear. Even if you go up to
the Boil it's very, very clear."
Manatees.
Blimps of the canal.
Zeppelins of warm water.
Loving dirigibles
(French for 'that which
can be guided).

Must I decide what I desire from a crane Lufthansa?
Should it be clear from the very first stanza?
I heard a naturalist say he loved to watch cranes dance.
I very much doubt he knew this in advance.

Especially when I consider the thoughtless age
when he first saw cranes drop and alight on a stage
as crowded as La Scala's chorus-ridden boards
when Verdi is sung to music-loving hordes.

Myself, I wouldn't say *dance* for the Sandhills.
Such interplay of feet, wings, breasts and bills
is for grebes that, when they begin to feel fond,
skim together a freshwater lake or pond.

When the tint of the sky is luminous but flat,
near the end of the sun and the start of the bat,
I think of tasteful, nature-themed wallpaper
and figures that drop to the floor and caper.

These are the Sandhills in mid-migration —
rude and teeming like Grand Central Station.
I also see them as airplanes sharing Blue.
Airplanes. Or pilots with dashing derring-do.

Villains or heroes? They have the same shape
to bipeds who shield their eyes, look up and gape.
Those flyers could drop bombs like B-52s —
or drop help civilians can actually use.

All of these scenes are made in my mind —
so much so, I would see them if I were blind.
Not only that — there is a further disgrace:
mixing up cranes with the human race.

As for those thousands that fly in mid-winter
and pause to feed in shallows in the center
of my country, a part that I've never seen — they
descended and danced tonight on this screen.

Occasional Poem

P is for poem, as in occasional.
Specifically this urban pastoral,
commissioned not for the
coronation of a queen but for the
coronation parade of all Queens.
I'm proud that the impulse,
the practicality, the public
spiritedness of this piece
rained on me in the shower one
morning six weeks ago when
I was soaping up my privates
and thinking of this podium.
I'm proud of the poem's presumptions —
I'm even proud of its imperfections.
P is for pre-parade. The years
before the very first march.
For each country that marches,
the years before their first.
Me in San Francisco, 1993 on
Market Street 30 minutes before
the Grand Marshal. The crowd made a
music like an orchestra tuning up.
People milled around like
galactic detritus which gravity was
about to pull into a world, a
planet bound to abound with life.
Me, deep in that silence I fall
into when I'm on the precipice of
a sublime decree. At last a

rumbling from the north
end of Market, the nervous
stomach of an unpredictable giant.
The tuning burst into overture.
The curtain rose on bike after
bike — motor upon motor —
Harleys guided by bachelor women,
Harleys bearing couples whom
the long road had wed — some
with breasts bared — some baring
victorious flesh where a breast
once breathed. These riders,
these leather Valkyries — their
staggering number combined
with the sudden knowing that I
loved them made me cry the
way I cry at weddings, the way I will
cry cradling the winner's bouquet as
Burt Parks declares me Mr. Poetry USA.
I'm proud five nights a week,
snuggling on the sofa watching
Rachel Maddow. Proud that
Mike and I both wear the pants
in this house. Just as proud if
one or both of us wore the panties.
I was proud the first time Mike
corrected the desk clerk at the
Hyatt Regency, "No, just one
bed. That's all we need." I was
proud and helplessly grateful
when aunts and cousins started
addressing Christmas cards and
invitations not to me but to us.

I'm proud that I can pronounce
the Vietnamese names of his
nieces and nephews, even if I can't
get the tones right. I'm as proud
as they were when, seeing a selfie
of him in his academic regalia,
they asked if he was graduating
from kindergarten. P is for private
first class. For Priapus and
Penelope and the promise that
someday I'll have a girl pal by that
name. I made that promise years
ago when it was hopelessly
unlikely. Now I know: No power
on earth, no prig in the skies,
no president on a purple throne,
no proctor at life's exam, no
'possum perched on a poplar
branch trying to make us say,
"Yes sir and no ma'am" will
keep us apart. I'm proud to
come up with songs off the cuff.
To be paid in applause and
know it's not enough. Proud
of the big cop in the park on a
horse that never uses brutal
force. Proud of those who take
care of their people, who know
their lives, who wait for
promotions that never arrive.
Proud of soldiers whispering
and giggling like 5th grade
kids rifling through dirty playing

cards. The clacking of hooves
bouncing a carriage over cobblestone
makes them snap their fingers loud
as firecrackers — makes them
laugh like fools who've lost
their laugh-blockers. I'm proud
of the savior across the tracks
giving away kindness she never gets
back, oblivious to her own ocean-deep
mercy. I'm proud that Mike and
I produced twenty years of
partnership [snap] just like that.
Each year a new child in our clan
of time (20 — reminiscent of
Bach's progeny. P is for prolific).
Year one, we dug a tunnel for
the BART and flooded it with
whispers. Two, we piled our
pasts into pillow cases and slung
them over our shoulders come
Christmas Eve. Three, we looked
back on our first quarrels like
an old couple rewriting an ancient
honeymoon. Four, our love-making
reached a pitch it won't reach again.
Five, like aging sopranos we
began replacing high notes with
sincerity. Six, we planted passwords
in Westwood's petite cinemas.
Later it was his job to remind us:
"That's where you lost your wallet."
"Bored by M. Night Shyamalan, it
was trying to escape." "That's

where the old woman played footsie
with you through the trailers. "In a
world that frowned on a fetish,
only she could accomplish…"
[growled like a trailer voiceover].
Seven, at the Fox Theater with its
pretentious back-lot spire, we
crashed a premier pretending
to be Press. Eight, he went to France
without me. Two months of flies in
the dormitory, feeding on a solitude
greater than any passion Paris had
ever ignored. Nine, in his dream,
we were boys in Hanoi, eating
sweetcorn on the street, climbing
trees at the zoo, peeing under our
desks in the classroom, running
naked through a nation's doom.
Ten, I rode in a taxi without him.
The paranoid cabbie dropped
me off at the foot of a hill that
became a mountain as I climbed it.
Eleven, when I reached the top I
 knew I was no one and would remain
no one till, twelve, a merciful Roc
seized and bore me back. Thirteen,
in the ER he brushed the nurse
aside, took me in hand and
aimed me at the pan. Fourteen, I
sat through two years of Unitarian
services, animals, on occasion,
wailing in my ears, preaching
at cross purposes while he waited

in the car, rehearsing for a Tourette's
audition, wondering what was
taking so long. Fifteen, We shined
a thin hot light in soup kitchen
corners. Sixteen, I painted the
walls with portraits of every
King, Count and Duke of the
Weather. Seventeen, he covered
the floor with the Number God's
paper trail. Eighteen, we won
the respect of towels and spies
and doctored photos and soldiers
turned student, and immigrant
mothers ready to hand over respect
the instant they walked into a
classroom. Nineteen, our auto
insurance grew restless. Twenty,
we took out life insurance policies
for ten bucks a month. P is for
privacy embodied in his mother's
daily sutra recitals behind a
paper mâché partition. P is for
pugilistic, which is how my
mom sounds when she says to
a church lady, "My oldest son
is married to a woman who
makes him smile, something
none of us could ever do,
and my youngest son is married
to a man I know will take
care of him when I'm gone."
P is for periphery where we no
longer dwell. P is for plain —

the day when joint bank
accounts sitting side by side
in lawn chairs with tired seats,
nodding at joggers and strollers
that compete for the Lake's
edge will be too ordinary to
merit the desperate word *Pride*.